ANCIENT EGYPT

 *Gods & Goddesses*

This book belongs to

_____

_____

Pensive Lines is a modern name for creative content creation. Here are connected skilled artists who design coloring books, various activity books and educational books for kids and adults. It can help boost confidence and make us feel more engaged and resilient. At the same time, we strongly encourage the creative freedom of our writers to collectively develop the talents of all to build a colorful and joyful world.

Feel free to check us out

Have questions? Let us know.

pensivelines@gmail.com

Copyright © by Pensive Lines

All Rights Reserved.

No part of this publication may be reproduced, distributed, or transmitted in any form or by any means, including photocopying, recording, or other electronic or mechanical methods, without the prior written permission of the publisher, except in the case of brief quotations embodied in critical reviews and certain other noncommercial uses permitted by copyright law.

Read This Before You Start!
This book contains hand-drawn and exclusive images only. Enjoy!

Creative Therapy
Coloring is an activity that is perfect to relax and avoid stress. You can fully use your creativity, **there are no rules.** You can do it by clearing completely your mind, also while listening to music, watching television, or just resting. There will be some images you will like more and some less, but the most important thing is that you enjoy the activity!

Tools Advice
The paper used by Amazon is most suitable for soft colored pencils. If you use them, be sure to keep them sharp so you can get a better result in every detail. If you prefer to use markers, gel pens, or similar, we suggest placing an extra blank paper sheet behind your page to avoid any bleed-through which might happen. You can even take your page out of the book if you want (the pages are NOT perforated, but you can find on Amazon a tool called a page perforator for under US$ 4).

Colors Choice
We prepared for you a **color test page** at the beginning of the book. Try out this page of your colors and find the better combination. We advise testing every time the colors you want to use as sometimes they can appear in a different way on paper than what you can expect.

Experience
If you come to an image you don't feel suitable to be colored at this moment, leave it there, you can pick it again another day! We recommend practicing every day, it helps to be more relaxing each time.

Sharing
Please **share your work,** it's nice to see how great are you. You can use Facebook Groups or Instagram, just don't forget to mention 'Pensive Lines' to **inspire other people** to take this book!

We hope you have fun and enjoy this book!
If you do, please consider writing positive feedback on Amazon which can be very helpful to support our artistic work and the publication of other books for you!

COLOR TEST PAGE

"Anubis"

Protector of the Dead

Anubis is shown as a jackal-headed man, or as a jackal. His father was Seth and his mother Nephythys. His cult center was Cynopolis, now known as El Kes. He was closely associated with mummification and as protector of the dead. It was Anubis who conducted the deceased to the hall of judgment.

"Bastet"

Bastet was the goddess of protection, pleasure, and the bringer of good health. She had the head of a cat and a slender female body. Bastet was the daughter of Ra, sister of Sekhmet, the wife of Ptah, and the mother of Mihos. Since the Second Dynasty, Bastet was worshiped as a deity, most commonly in Lower Egypt.

"Ra"

Ra was the king of the deities and the father of all creation. He was the patron of the sun, heaven, kingship, power, and light. He was not only the deity who governed the actions of the sun, he could also be the physical sun itself, as well as the day.

"Tefnut"

Tefnut (tfnwt) is a deity of moisture, moist air, dew and rain in Ancient Egyptian religion. She is the sister and consort of the air god Shu and the mother of Geb and Nut. The goddess Tefnut portrayed as a woman with the head of a lioness and a sun disc resting on her head.

"Seth"

Seth, or Set, Ancient Egyptian god and patron of the 11th nome, or province, of Upper Egypt. A trickster, he was a sky god, lord of the desert, and master of storms, disorder, and warfare. He was the brother of Osiris, whom he killed, and he was antagonistic to Horus, the child of Osiris's sister, Isis.

"Sobek"

He was the lord of the crocodiles and was depicted with a crocodile head. Some ancient Egyptian sects believed that Sobek created order in the universe and the world when he arose from the "Dark Water" and that he was the creator of the Nile River. He was often associated with fertility.

"Hathor"

Hathor, in ancient Egyptian religion, goddess of the sky, of women, and of fertility and love. Hathor's worship originated in early dynastic times (3rd millennium bce). The name Hathor means "estate of Horus" and may not be her original name.

"Hapi"

Hapi (Ancient Egyptian: ḥʿpy) was the god of the annual flooding of the Nile in ancient Egyptian religion. The flood deposited rich silt (fertile soil) on the river's banks, allowing the Egyptians to grow crops. Hapi was greatly celebrated among the Egyptians.

"Ma'at"

Ma'at is the Egyptian goddess of truth and justice. She is married to Thoth and is the daughter of Ra, the sun god. In addition to truth, she embodies harmony, balance, and divine order. In Egyptian legends, it is Ma'at who steps in after the universe is created, and brings harmony amidst the chaos and disorder.

"Osiris"

Osiris, one of Egypt's most important deities, was god of the underworld. He also symbolized death, resurrection, and the cycle of Nile floods that Egypt relied on for agricultural fertility. According to the myth, Osiris was a king of Egypt who was murdered and dismembered by his brother Seth.

"Geb"

Geb was believed to be the deity of earth, and was central to the ancient Egyptian creation myth. In fact, the ancient Egyptians referred to Earth as the "House of Geb." According to the ancient Egyptians, Geb was the grandson of Ra, and the son of Shu and Tefnut, the deities of air and moisture, respectively.

"Isis"

Isis was the ancient Egyptian goddess of fertility and was also known as the goddess of motherhood, magic, death, healing, and rebirth. Isis was the first daughter of Geb and Nut who was the god of the earth and the goddess of the sky. Isis was the sister of Osiris who later on became her husband as well.

"Shu"

Shu, in Egyptian religion, god of the air and supporter of the sky, created by Atum by his own power, without the aid of a woman. Shu and his sister and companion, Tefnut (goddess of moisture), were the first couple of the group of nine gods called the Ennead of Heliopolis.

"Montu"

Montu was a falcon-god of war in ancient Egyptian religion, an embodiment of the conquering vitality of the pharaoh. He was particularly worshipped in Upper Egypt and in the district of Thebes.

"Mut"

Mut was usually represented as a woman wearing the double crown (of Upper and Lower Egypt) typically worn by the king and by the god Atum. She was also occasionally depicted with the head of a lioness, particularly when identified with other goddesses, principally Bastet and Sekhmet.

"Amun"

Amun, god of the air, was one of the eight primordial Egyptian deities. Amun's role evolved over the centuries; during the Middle Kingdom he became the King of the deities and in the New Kingdom he became a nationally worshipped god. He eventually merged with Ra, the ancient sun god, to become Amun-Ra.

"Nephthys"

Nephthys, or "Mistress of the House," was the goddess of the air (since the sky is the "head" of the world) and the head of the family. She also sometimes represented Lower Egypt along with Ptah-Tanen. In Egyptian mythology, Nephthys was the daughter of Geb (Earth) and Nut (sky) and the sister of Isis.

"Thoth"

Thoth, (Greek), Egyptian Djhuty, in Egyptian religion, a god of the moon, of reckoning, of learning, and of writing. He was held to be the inventor of writing, the creator of languages, the scribe, interpreter, and adviser of the gods, and the representative of the sun god, Re.

"Horus"

Horus or Heru, Hor, Har in Ancient Egyptian, is one of the most significant ancient Egyptian deities who served many functions, most notably as the god of kingship and the sky. He was worshipped from at least late prehistoric Egypt until the Ptolemaic Kingdom and Roman Egypt.

"Nut"

Nut was the mother of Osiris, Isis, Seth, and Nephthys, Nut is usually shown in human form; her elongated body symbolizes the sky. Each limb represents a cardinal point as her body stretches over the earth. Nut swallowed the setting sun (Ra) each evening and gave birth to him each morning. She is often depicted on the ceilings of tombs, on the inside lid of coffins, and on the ceilings of temples.

"Khnum"

Khnum, was depicted as a ram-headed man. He was a god of the cataracts, a potter, and a creator god who guarded the source of the Nile,. His sanctuary was on Elephantine Island but his best-preserved temple is at Esna. The "Famine Stele", which is a carved stone tablet, contains appeals to Khnum during a famine caused by a low inundation of the Nile.

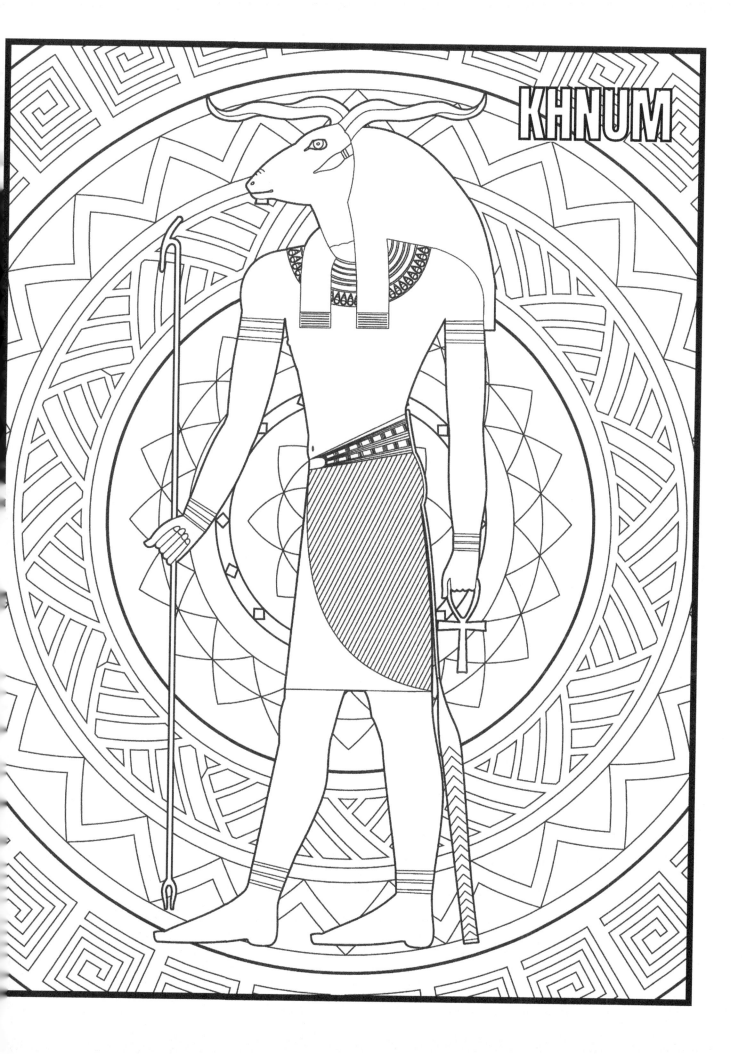

"Seshat"

Seshat, Ancient Egyptian: sš3t, under various spellings, was the ancient Egyptian goddess of writing, wisdom, and knowledge. She was seen as a scribe and record keeper; her name means "female scribe". She is credited with inventing writing.

"Khonsu"

Khonsu, also known as Khons or Khensu, was the Egyptian god of the moon, Time, Youth, and healing. He is the son of Amun and is also associated with Thoth and Iah. He can take the appearance of Iah. It is believed that at the beginning of times, Thoth was the god of the moon.

"Selket"

Selket, also spelled Selqet, or Serqet, in Egyptian mythology, goddess of the dead. Her symbolic animal was the scorpion. She was one of the underworld deities charged with protecting the canopic jar in which the intestines of the deceased were stored after embalming.

"Ptah"

Ptah, also spelled Phthah, in Egyptian religion, creator-god and maker of things, a patron of craftsmen, especially sculptors; his high priest was called "chief controller of craftsmen." The Greeks identified Ptah with Hephaestus (Vulcan), the divine blacksmith.

"khepri"

Also known as, Khepri, Khepra, Khepera, Khepre was a creator god depicted as a Scarab beetle or as a man with a scarab for a head. The Egyptians observed young scarab beetles emerging spontaneously from balls of dung and associated them with the process of creation. Khepre was one of the first gods, self-created, and his name means "he who has come into being," Atum took his form as he rose out of the chaotic waters of the Nun in a creation myth. It was thought that Khepre rolled the sun across the sky in the same way a dung beetle rolls balls of dung across the ground.

"Ammit"

In Egyptian Mythology, Ammit is actually more of a creature than a god. She is known as the devourer of souls and participates in the important Egyptian ceremony, the weighing of the heart. Egyptians believed that after death, the scales of Ma'at, the goddess of truth and justice, judged every person's heart .

"Taweret"

Taweret, after all, was a god of fertility, of life. And life was better than the alternative. For a time, there were even several overlapping hippo deities in ancient Egypt. Ipet, Reret, and Hedjet all played essentially the same role as Taweret, and may even have been aspects of the same deity.

"Bes"

Bes is the ancient Egyptian god of childbirth, fertility, sexuality, humor, and war, but served primarily as a protector god of pregnant women and children. He is regularly depicted as a dwarf with large ears, long-haired and bearded, with prominent genitals, and bow-legged.

Made in the USA
Coppell, TX
27 November 2022